The Principle of Order

By:
Christian Gómez

Published by Melanin Origins

PO Box 122123; Arlington, TX 76012

All rights reserved, including the right of reproduction in whole

or in part in any form.

Copyright 2022

First Edition

The author asserts the moral right under the Copyright, Designs and Patents Act of 1988 to be identified as the author of this work.

This novel is a work of fiction. The names, characters and incidents portrayed in the work, other than those clearly in the public domain, are of the author's imagination and are not to be construed as real. Any resemblance to actual persons, living or dead, events or localities, is entirely coincidental.

All rights reserved. No part of this publication may be reproduced, stored in a retrieval system or transmitted, in any form by any means without the prior consent of the author, nor be otherwise circulated in any form of binding or cover other than that with which it is published and without a similar condition being imposed on the subsequent purchaser.

Library of Congress Control Number: 2021942165

ISBN: 978-1-62676-516-0 hardback

ISBN: 978-1-62676-517-7 paperback

ISBN: 978-1-62676-518-4 ebook

The Principle of Order

"I respect the natural order of the divinely governed universe; I will not separate myself from that which gives order to the world."

www.MelaninOrigins.com

Although he loved puzzles, one day he ran into a problem he felt was too confusing for him to solve while working on a jigsaw puzzle his parents gave him for his birthday.

"Well then, what do you see when you look at the puzzle pieces on the floor?" His mother questioned. Isaiah lifted his hands and said, "A big mess."

Giggling as she pointed to the puzzle pieces, Isaiah's mother said, "That's because there is no order, so, all we can see is clutter. To complete the puzzle, you have to clear your mind to place everything in order." She said.

Order simply means to arrange things in a special pattern or design that makes sense." His mother explained.

The Creator made the Sun to give us light in the day, the Moon to shine the way for us at night, and the Creator gave us fresh water to flow from the ocean to the rivers down to our home so we can bathe and drink refreshing water each day. There is an order to just about everything.

Isaiah started to think hard about what his mother said. "Can you give me another hint?" He asked while slightly chuckling.

"I sure can, what do you think belongs at the top of the puzzle?" She asked.

Isaiah picked up a few pieces and said, "The sky!"

His mother smiled. "That's right because the sky is above the mountains, the trees, and the lions! Okay, now piece the sky together where you think it fits best."

After Isaiah perfectly matched the pieces of the sky, he rejoiced. "Wow! I think I'm getting somewhere!"

"You see that! All you had to do was clear your mind to discover the order. It looks like you got it from here. Keep going, your father and I will watch!" Mom said.

"You are on a roll son!" Isaiah's father said.

"And last but not least we have the mommy lion to the right, the son lion in the middle, and the daddy lion sitting comfortably in the grass!" Isaiah said as he attached the final pieces to the jigsaw puzzle. "I did it! I'm all finished!"

Isaiah's parents started clapping. "Yay!" they cheered.

"Now that you completed the puzzle, we can clearly see the lion family enjoying themselves in nature." Isaiah's mother said.

"You're welcome sweetheart! Now help me put these pieces back in the box." Isaiah's mother said as she began to tickle him.

"Sure thing mom! Once we put the puzzle pieces away, I will help you prepare the table for dinner; setting each piece of tableware in its proper place."

Modern Day Melanin Origins

This book is dedicated to the fond remembrance and blessed, loving memory of Master Teacher **Dr. John Henrik Clarke**.

Dr. John Henrik Clarke, January 1, 1915 - July 16, 1998, was a Pan-Africanist writer, historian, professor, and a pioneer in the creation of Africana Studies in professional institutions and academia.

The greatest period of his influence resides in the 1960's where he was a **prominent intellectual** during the Black Power Movement, advocating studies on the African-American experience and the place of Africans in world history. **Dr. Clark** challenged the views of academic historians and **helped shift** the way African history was studied and taught.

~ BlackHistoryMonth.org.uk

www.ingramcontent.com/pod-product-compliance
Lightning Source LLC
Chambersburg PA
CBHW040013080526
44586CB00028B/2989